The Great Trek

The Burke and Wills Story

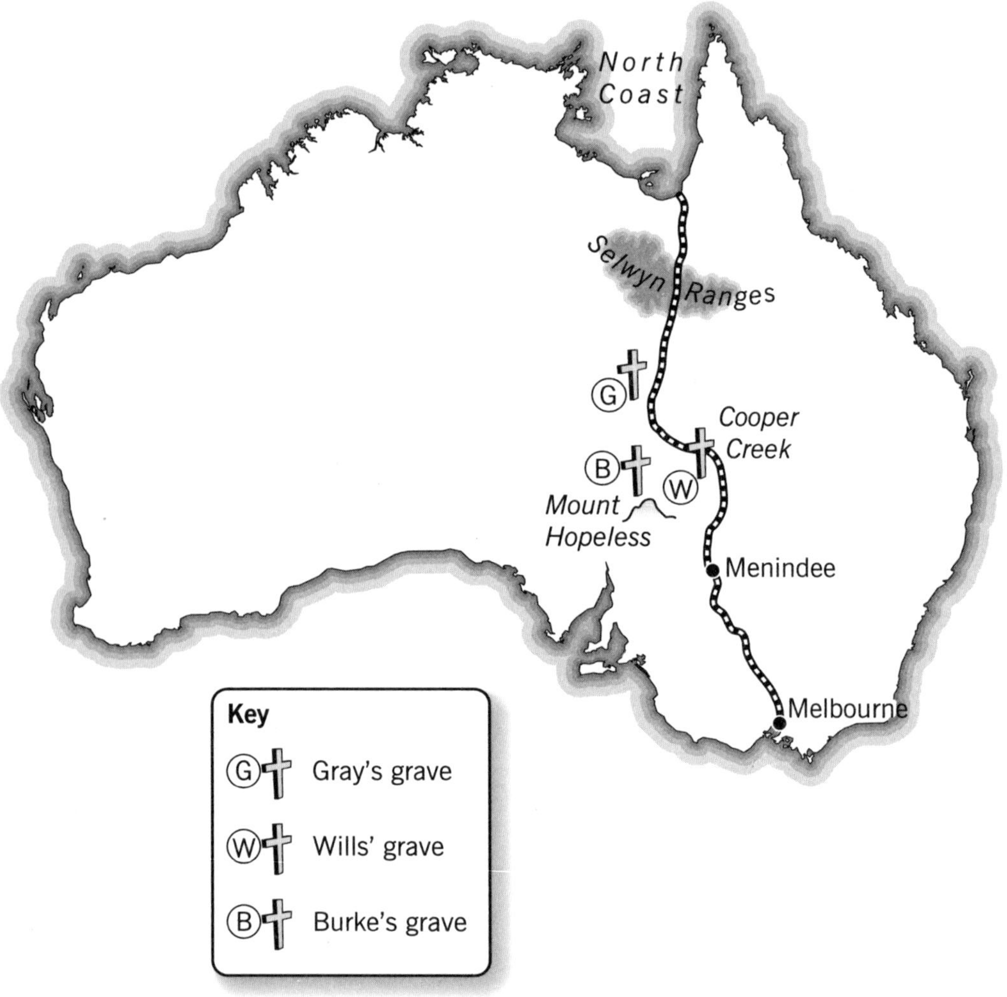
North
Coast
Selwyn
Ranges
Cooper
Creek
G
B
W
Mount
Hopeless
Menindee
Melbourne
Key
G Gray's grave
W Wills' grave
B Burke's grave

NEW Spirals

NON-FICTION

The Great Trek
The Burke and Wills Story

James Rigg

Published in 2004 by:
Nelson Thornes Ltd
Delta Place
27 Bath Road
CHELTENHAM
GL53 7TH
United Kingdom

04 05 06 07 08 / 10 9 8 7 6 5 4 3 2 1

A catalogue record for this book is available from the British Library

ISBN 0 7487 9005 5

Cover illustration by Gordon Lawson
Page make-up by Tech-Set, Gateshead

Printed in Croatia by Zrinski

Introduction

On Monday 20 August 1860, 19 men set out to cross Australia. Some people thought they were fools. To others, they were heroes. No white man had ever crossed Australia before.

Most Australian towns were on the coast. Some men had gone a little way inland. Places like Menindee and Cooper Creek were out in the wilds. But at least they were on the map.

From Cooper Creek a vast desert rolled into the distance. No white man had crossed the desert before. No one knew what lay on the far side . . . or if they'd get back.

This book can't tell the tale of all 19 men. It tells of just seven of them. Some lived. Some paid with their lives.

The man you'll hear most about is **Robert Burke.** He was the leader of the group. His second in command was **George Landells**. Landells' place was taken later by **William Wills.** It was Burke, Wills and two other men – **John King** and **Charlie Gray** – who made the great trek north.

Burke also had a back-up team. Their job was to make sure of the food and supplies back at camp. **William Brahe** was one of these men. Another was a bushman called **William Wright.** There was another group who helped the explorers. They knew how to survive under a hot sun. They were the **Australian Aborigines**.

The Great Trek shows that men can be brave as well as foolish. It is a tale of adventure and of sadness. People risked their lives for a dream.

Above all it's the story of man's need to explore.

1

Melbourne, Australia 1860

News used to take months to travel across Australia. To speed up the news, telegraph wires were needed. They'd have to cross the country. But there was a problem. No white man had ever crossed Australia. Most Australians lived by the sea. No one knew what lay in the middle of the country.

There might be strange animals. There might be a great lake. There might be cities. And tribes who'd never seen a white man. The only way to find out was to explore.

Someone had to be found to do the job. He'd have to find the best place for a telegraph line. The line had to run from the south of Australia to the north. At the same time he'd explore the country. A competition was set up to find the best person. The man chosen was Robert Burke.

Burke was born in Ireland. He'd been in the army there. After the army he joined the police. Later, he left Ireland and moved to Australia. He became a policeman in Melbourne. Melbourne is a city in SE Australia.

Burke liked police work. But sometimes it was boring. He wanted to do more with his life. Exploring Australia might give him fame and fortune.

But there was a problem. Exploring a new country takes a lot of skill. You have to be ready when things go wrong. You have to plan. You have to know what to take and what to leave. Burke had never explored anything before. He knew nothing about leading a team. He'd even got lost coming home from the pub.

He was hard. He loved life. He wanted adventure. But was that enough to cross an unknown land and stay alive?

Burke would not be put off. He wanted to be the first white man to cross Australia. Or he'd die trying.

His first job was to get a team together. He chose 19 men. They had to be men he could trust.

Each man had a job to do. No one knew what they'd find on the trip. A man's life could be in the hands of his mate. And in case anything happened to Burke, he needed a second in command. A man named George Landells was chosen.

The next problem was transport. Food and stores had to be carried a long, long way. In 1860 there were no Land Rovers. No trucks. But there were horses, wagons and camels. Burke put Landells in charge of the camels.

From the start, Burke and Landells didn't see eye to eye. Burke was sure they could cross Australia. Landells thought they might die trying. For a start, the team would have to walk 5,000km from coast to coast. That was like going from London to Moscow and back. And they could only move slowly as there were big loads to carry. Then there was the problem of food. If it ran out, would they find food away from the Australian coast?

Burke didn't like Landells arguing with him. He didn't like Landells. Landells didn't like Burke. And that wasn't good for the team.

2

20 August 1860
The Journey Begins

The big day came. The team were ready. The starting place was a park in Melbourne. Cameras popped. People came to cheer and wave them off.

But things didn't look good. Heavy rain had fallen. The park was full of mud. It wasn't long before the wagons got stuck. One even broke down. Then more rain came down. But not enough to dampen their spirits. At last they were on the move.

They did no more than 11km the first day. They moved very slowly. They had 26 camels, 23 horses and six loaded wagons. The team had to learn as they went along. They spent their time pushing the wagons and shouting at the camels to move them on.

They'd only got to the edge of Melbourne by nightfall. Things were not going well. They had to unpack, but nobody knew where anything was. Or who was in charge of what. Burke was the boss. But he didn't know what to do either. He got angry and swore at the men. He told them he'd nail troublemakers to a tree by their ears. It took a long time to set up camp.

As Burke was about to turn in for the night, he saw a figure in the darkness. It was a man called Dr Wills. He had a son called William. William was one of Burke's team. Dr Wills had tears in his eyes.

'If I could stop my son going, I would,' he said. 'But I can't. He's a good lad. You can trust him with your life. I only ask one thing.'

Burke asked him what it was.

'Please bring my son back alive,' came the reply.

The man walked off into the night. Burke began to think about William Wills. He was very keen. He was very bright. He was a scientist. He'd always wanted to explore. He'd told his mother he was not afraid to die. Burke knew this when he'd made Wills part of the team. He hoped he could bring William back alive. He knew he could trust Wills.

There was another man in the team he could trust, too. That man was John King.

The three of them would live to see the north coast. Burke was sure of it. With these thoughts buzzing in his head, he fell asleep.

3

Heading North

They set off late next morning. It had taken a long time to pack. The team dragged slowly past the houses north of Melbourne. More rain fell. The roads were a sea of mud. Then there were hailstones as big as billiard balls.

At night it was frosty. Their water froze in their billicans. Burke took no notice. He just pressed on.

The first week passed. They were now 100km from Melbourne. They'd had plenty of rain but no tea and no fire. They slept in the wet. No one was happy. They began to fall out with each other. Some of the men even left.

Burke had a problem on his hands. His team was already falling apart. He decided to split the team in two. He went ahead with a smaller group. He took some of the camels and horses with him.

He hoped to make better time that way.

Some bushmen showed him the best way north. Burke wouldn't listen. He wanted to take a short cut.

His plan was a disaster. He found himself trying to cross sand hills. The roots of Mallee trees blocked his way.

Things got even harder. Now the horses had to pull the wagons through a wild land. The wagons sank into deep earth. The horses sank up to their knees. The horses were worn out. As if that wasn't enough, strong winds blew in the night. The tents flew into the air. Some were ripped apart.

In the end the horses were too tired to pull the wagons. Burke told Landells the camels would have to bear the load. But Landells didn't want his camels loaded down yet. They'd need all their strength later on. The two men had a row. It was clear they wouldn't be working together long.

Camels weren't the only thing Burke and Landells had words about. Landells had brought a lot of rum along. He said it was for the animals. Burke didn't believe him. He thought Landells might sell the rum and make a lot of money. The two men began to argue about the rum. The row went on till sunset.

That night, some men broke into the stores. They helped themselves to the rum. The newspapers got hold of the story. It made Burke feel a fool. Did he have no control over what was happening? He told

Landells to leave the rest of the rum behind. Landells said no. They fell out again. And while they were shouting at each other, the camels ran off.

Burke ordered his men to look for them. They didn't find a single one. He was forced to pay an Aborigine tracker to look for them. The tracker soon found the animals.

The men said Landells was hopeless with camels. He had to show them they were wrong. He had to prove himself. Now he drove the camels day and night. He made them run. They came to the edge of a vast desert. By now the camels were worn out.

Landells expected another row with Burke. But Landells had a row with William Wills instead. Wills told him he'd be taking over as second in command.

Landells stormed off to find Burke. The two began to have another row.

'Sacked am I? On whose orders?' shouted Landells.

'Mine,' shouted Burke.

'You're mad,' cried Landells.

'Mad am I?' said Burke. 'I don't like being called mad. Take back your words.'

'I won't,' cried Landells.

'Then we'll shoot it out,' Burke replied. 'With pistols.'

'I'm not in the mood,' shouted Landells, and stormed off.

The next morning, the team got to a river. Burke tied a rope to each camel. He wanted them to swim across the river. He wanted to save time.

'I'm in charge of the camels,' yelled Landells. 'They'll all drown. I say they cross the river by boat.'

'I say they're swimming,' Burke replied. 'You've run all the fat off them. They'll swim across, no problem.'

Burke was right for once. The camels swam across the river.

'I told you they'd swim,' he said. 'You don't know the first thing about camels.'

Landells went mad. He packed his bags and went back to Melbourne. Burke was pleased. Now William Wills could have Landells' job. Wills wouldn't argue as Landells had done.

The team had gone 750km in 56 days. They were about to go into the unknown. Burke looked out over the hills of sand.

'I'll get there,' he said to himself. 'Nothing will stop me.'

4

The Team Split Up

Day by day the explorers moved north. The sun burnt in a blue sky. They reached a place called Menindee. They learned from the Aborigines that there was water there. But they got there at the wrong time of year. The heat had dried up most of the waterholes. They had to make do with a little dirty water.

Some of them thought they should stay in Menindee until the hot season was over. They'd travel again when it was cooler. But Burke was against the idea. He thought they might start to row, or split up. Or they might get bored and go back to Melbourne.

He didn't want to wait three more months. He didn't want a rival to beat him. He wanted to be the first man to cross Australia.

He decided to carry on, come what may. He chose seven men to go with him into the desert. He left the rest in Menindee. He was taking a chance. Much of the food would be in Menindee while he and the other seven would be in the desert. If he needed more food, how would he get it?

He took his best men. Men he could trust. He took Wills and King with him. He now put King in charge of the camels. Then he took on a man called William Wright. Wright was a bushman. He knew the ways of the desert. Burke also hired two Aborigines from a local tribe. They'd learned to survive in the desert. They knew how to find food and water in the sand.

The group began to make good progress. But the land was as dry as a bone. Wills was worried they'd run out of water. But Burke was in too much of a rush to worry. He didn't even stop at water holes. It might slow him down. If they spotted one in the afternoon he'd just pass by. He made his team march 16 hours a day. It didn't matter how thirsty they got.

But in the end even Burke had to stop for water. They'd reached some mountains. Between the mountains were deep valleys. In the valleys were dark pools of good water. They filled their water bags.

If they hadn't come across the pools, they'd have died of thirst.

5

Cooper Creek

On 11 November 1860, the group reached a place called Cooper Creek. They were half way across Australia. Again they were lucky. Some years the creek was dry. Nothing would live near it. But when they got there it was full of water.

Burke and Wills watched turtles and water rats in the creek. They saw snakes with enough poison to kill 100 men. Luckily, the snakes didn't go near the explorers.

An Aborigine tribe lived around the creek. They worried that the explorers would take all their water. The tribe had never seen camels or wagons before. The tribes people were shocked by the sunburned white men.

The tribe tried to ask them where they were from and what they wanted. Burke couldn't understand what they were trying to say. He was worried the tribe might attack him. He shot over their heads.

He didn't try to understand these people. If he had, the team could have found out what plants to eat and what to leave. They missed their chance. They didn't think the tribe could help them.

William Wright and the two guides went back to Menindee. They'd taken the explorers as far as they knew. Burke asked Wright to bring fresh horses and food back to Cooper Creek.

Burke and Wills watched Wright and the guides fade into the desert. Now they were alone at Cooper Creek. They had water and a little food. Hardly enough to see them through the next part of their journey.

6

Into the Unknown

Burke asked Wills to spend a day looking for a way north. Burke would wait at Cooper Creek for him to get back. Wills took two camels and rode into the desert. He took another man with him. The other man was called Thomas McDonaugh.

The sun beat down. The heat got to the two men. They were soon low on water. The camels grew tired. The men decided to rest. They didn't tie up the camels. The camels ran off across the desert. Wills and McDonough had to walk back to the camp in the burning heat.

They were lucky. They found water holes. There was just enough water left to drink. It was thick and green. But they still drank some of it. They filled their water bags.

It took two days to get back to Cooper Creek. They'd walked 115km in the boiling sun. When they got back to camp they only had a drop of water left. The two men had almost died in the desert.

Back at Cooper Creek, rats had become a problem. They ate boot leather and they ate the food. They chewed the men's hair as they slept. They even chewed the explorers' toenails.

Burke couldn't wait any longer. He was in a rush to move on. He decided to carry on with just three men. They were Wills, King and a man called Charley Gray. Burke wanted another man, William Brahe, to stay behind.

'I want you to wait at Cooper Creek for three months,' he said to Brahe. 'If we don't come back in three months, take the rest of the men back to Menindee.'

Burke had already told William Wright to return to Cooper Creek with fresh supplies. He thought he'd covered everything. With that, Burke, Wills, King and Gray headed into the unknown. By December 1860, they were 200km from the creek. December is one of the hottest months in Australia.

They made very slow progress through the desert. They marched 12 hours a day. They didn't have enough food or water. The sun beat down on them every day. They grew weak. Their hair became brittle. Their skin flaked off. Their nails began to crack. Their hands and feet split open. Flies attacked them as they slept. They wouldn't survive long without food and water.

Again, luck was on their side. They found a river. If they'd gone slightly west they would've missed it. They got to a creek. Now there was water to drink. They saw pelicans and kangaroos, too. That meant food to eat.

They'd survived the desert. Now the land was changing. It was hilly. The air was still hot. But it was damp, too. And there were some trees.

Burke and his team had reached another part of Australia. A part that white men had never set eyes on before.

7

Journey's End

The men had reached some mountains. Now they're called the Selwyn Ranges. They had to drag their camels over the top. It was a hard job. It took them six days.

As they went on, they were watched by a fierce tribe of Aborigines called the Kalkadoons. The Kalkadoons painted their bodies and ate Kangaroo meat. The group didn't know the Kalkadoons wanted to kill them.

As they got ready to attack, the Kalkadoons noticed the camels. The tribe thought the camels and the white men were from the gods. They didn't dare attack them now.

The camels had saved the explorers from a horrible death.

At last the group crossed the Selwyn Ranges. They followed a river now known as the Cloncurry. They didn't know it, but they were less than 200km from the north coast.

Burke and his men had reached the point of no return. Food stocks were very low. They were now halfway through the three months Brahe was told to wait for them. But Burke wouldn't be put off.

'I'll reach the sea even if I get there with no shirt on my back,' he told the others. 'I'll get to the end or I'll die trying. There's no turning back.'

Every day the men moved north. Further and further from Cooper Creek. Further and further from safety. Food was short. They were dragging themselves along. But Burke wouldn't give in.

At last the 4 men reached the tropics. They got there just before the rainy season. The heat was worse than ever. Night was as hot as day.

They lay on their bedrolls. Mosquitoes bit them. Their food began to rot in the heat. The leather straps for the camels and horses turned mouldy.

One of the camels saw a creek and climbed down. It wanted to drink the water. It couldn't get back up again. It got stuck. The four men couldn't pull it out. Burke decided to leave the camel. Now they only had four camels left.

They came to a dense wood of small trees. They couldn't make the camels go through the trees. They'd almost reached the northern coast.

Burke and Wills left King and Gray with the camels and headed for the coast. But it wasn't easy going. Before long the two men came to a vast swamp. They knew they could go no further. They couldn't see the sea. But they'd reached the coast. Journey's end.

They'd walked from south to north Australia. People had said it couldn't be done. But they'd done it. They'd proved there were no lost cities in the middle of Australia. They knew there were no inland lakes. There were no new beasts. Just desert and sand. And in the north, hot wet forests and swamps. Now they had to get back to Melbourne and tell the world what they'd found out.

First, they had to get back to Cooper Creek. If their luck held, William Wright would have returned there from Menindee . . . with food and drink.

And maybe Brahe would still be there to greet them.

8

Meanwhile, Back at Cooper Creek...

As Burke and his small team were starting back south, William Brahe and his men were waiting at Cooper Creek. They were bored. There was nothing to do. At first the men had kept busy. They'd made a strong hut to keep food and supplies in. They'd also taken care of the animals. Each day one man would graze the horses. A second man would look after the camels. The other men would guard the store and collect firewood. They also fished and baked bread.

But each day was the same as the last. Time dragged. The creek was cut off on all sides by desert. The real world seemed far away.

Some Aborigines lived close to the creek. The Aborigines gave the explorers presents. Like fish and fish nets. But they stole cans and saddles. Brahe was afraid the tribe might attack him. He drew a line in the dirt. He tried to tell the tribe that nobody could cross the line. The tribes-people left, then came back. They had spears. They'd painted their bodies. They were angry.

Brahe fired shots over their heads. The Aborigines ran past the horses. They yelled and screamed. The horses bolted. Brahe ran after the Aborigines. He fired more shots over their heads.

Later, the Aborigines came back. They tried to make friends with the strangers. They offered more gifts. But Brahe wouldn't have them. It seemed like war. His men were now afraid to shoot duck or to fish from the creek in case the tribesmen started to fight them.

Brahe couldn't wait for the three months to pass. He looked south to see if William Wright was coming back to the creek with new supplies. He looked north to see if Burke and Wills were returning. He saw no one. Just hills of dust and sand that went on and on.

He felt as if Cooper Creek was a prison.

9

The End of Charlie Gray

While Brahe waited at Cooper Creek, Burke and his three men moved slowly south. Their walk back was harder than their journey north. They were tired. They had even less to eat. The most they could do was 7km a day. There was rain and storms. The camels were worn out. They dragged themselves through mud.

The party followed their own tracks back. They even found the lost camel. It was thin but alive. It must have managed to pull itself out of the creek.

They were still in the tropics. The rain and heat got them down. Burke was worried the horses might die.

He pushed the group on. He knew the food would run out before they made it to their stores at Cooper Creek. He'd hoped to find wild animals to hunt. But there were no wild animals. There was nothing to eat.

At meal times the explorers lined up. Burke would give them a plate. On the plate was some flour and a few sticks of rotting meat. They had to wave away the flies. They lost weight. They lost their strength.

As they marched south they dreamed of food. They dreamed of a perfect meal.

The first man to fall ill was Charley Gray. The rest of the group thought he was making things up. They all had to look after themselves. Gray was holding them back. They began to hate him.

As they were crossing the Selwyn Ranges, Wills found Gray eating food from the stores. All the men were hungry. They were mad at Gray. He'd lost their trust. Burke hit Gray for robbing them. The beating made Gray sick. He began to give up.

Now the group reached the desert. This time water was harder to find. The water holes had dried up. It was hotter than ever. The daytime heat was like an oven. At night it was so cold they all shivered. They were blasted by sandstorms and woke up covered in sand.

Their food was almost used up. The only thing to eat was a camel. Burke shot the weakest animal. That night they all ate camel meat. The next day Gray couldn't walk. They strapped him to a horse. The horse gave way under him. It had to be shot. That night the men ate horse meat.

The group were now losing hope. They knew Gray would die. He was slowing them down. This was putting them all in danger. They had to carry him or wait for him to catch up. Wills thought it was Gray's fault for being ill.

'He lived in a pub. I heard he drank a lot,' he said. 'He made himself ill through drink.'

Nine days later Charley Gray died. He'd spent his last days strapped to a camel. The three other men spent nine hours digging Gray a grave. They were too worn out to say a prayer.

Burke didn't want to go the same way as Charley Gray. He'd get back, come what may. He ordered his party to throw away everything but food. They had to reach Cooper Creek fast or die. Maybe Brahe and his men would still be waiting for them. Four months had passed by. He knew Brahe and his men should have left Cooper Creek after three months. But maybe, just maybe, he'd still be there.

On 21 April 1861 they staggered into Cooper Creek. They shouted out for Brahe and his men. There was no reply. They ran into Brahe's camp. It was empty.

King saw a campfire. He bent down to feel the ashes. They were still warm. Brahe and his men must have left earlier that day. The three men cursed their bad luck.

10

Missed Chances

Burke guessed they'd missed Brahe and his men by about nine hours. That was the same time it had taken to bury Gray. They should have left Gray on the sand. Then they'd have reached Cooper Creek before Brahe left.

Burke didn't want to stay at Cooper Creek. He'd done what he set out to do. Now he wanted to get back to Melbourne. And glory. Fast. He had a plan. He'd take another route back. He'd head for Mount Hopeless, 250km away. This was the outpost for the South Australian Police.

Wills and King begged him to follow the track they knew back to Menindee. But Burke wouldn't listen. He knew they had to cross more unknown places. He knew his plan was risky. But he thought it would be a short cut back to safety. In the end Wills and King gave in. They began to struggle towards Mount Hopeless . . .

At the same time, William Wright and his team had met up with Brahe. Both groups had had problems. Wright had trouble getting new supplies. Some of Brahe's men were ill.

Wright and Brahe decided to ride back to Cooper Creek in case Burke had now made it from the north.

When the two men reached Cooper Creek they saw no sign of life. They didn't know Burke, Wills and King had been there. They thought the Burke party had all died in the desert. They didn't know the three survivors were now walking south to Mount Hopeless.

Wills and King had been right. They'd have met Wright and Brahe if they'd followed their old track back.

They'd missed two chances of rescue.

11

Another Death

Burke and his party struggled on under a baking sun. They were almost out of food. It seemed they'd never reach Mount Hopeless. But Wills thought they'd survive if they lived off the land like the Aborigines.

He knew tribesmen made flour from a plant, the nardoo. Wills couldn't find any nardoo. He looked for it in the trees. He didn't know it grew in the ground. He thought he'd trap birds. But he had no nets.

He wanted to find Aborigine people to help him. But they were nowhere to be seen.

He knew that without help the team would die. He begged Burke to let him return to Cooper Creek. Wills wanted to find the camp where Brahe and his men had stayed. He'd kept a diary. He wanted to hide the diary under a tree. He wanted somebody to find it if the worse happened.

Wills didn't know Wright and Brahe had been back to the creek just days before. And left again.

The journey back almost killed Wills. But luckily some Aborigine people had given him food. He began to feel better. He got strong again because the Aborigines fed him. He felt strong enough to travel back to Burke and King.

When Wills got back to their camp he knew something was wrong. Burke and King had argued with the Aborigines for taking an old cloth in exchange for food. Burke had shot at a tribesman.

The tribe couldn't understand Burke. They'd given him a present of fish and nets. But if they wanted anything back he'd shoot at them. They went off again. The explorers no longer had food gifts. Now they were on their own.

Wills got angry with Burke. He knew the explorers couldn't survive without the help of the Aborigines. Burke lost his temper. He hit Wills and knocked him to the ground. The men were so worn out they didn't know what they were doing.

On 26 June Wills grew ill. He begged the other two to leave him. Burke was upset. He'd made friends with Wills again. He remembered Wills' father's words: 'Please bring my son back alive.'

But there was nothing Burke could do. He and King had to reach Mount Hopeless. It was their only chance.

Burke's eyes filled with tears. He knew he'd left Wills to die alone. He left Wills a can of water and a little food. He also left some wood for a fire.

Nobody knows when William Wills died. He was looking across at the desert as the other two left him. He was waiting for death to come.

12

Burke and King

Burke and King walked for a day. They still hoped someone would rescue them. By now Burke was tired and full of pain. He knew he could walk no longer. He knew he'd never make it to Mount Hopeless or Melbourne. He knew death would come to him, as it had come to Wills.

'When I'm dead don't bury me,' he whispered to King. 'Don't waste your strength.'

Burke died the next morning. King was left alone in the middle of the desert. He was 600km from the nearest town. There was only one thing to do. He made up his mind to go back to Wills. Perhaps Wills was still alive.

He dragged himself back over the sand. He found William Wills dead. Wild dogs had eaten some of his body. King covered the body with sand. He was too weak to bury his friend.

Then he had a stroke of luck. A friendly tribe found him. They saw how ill he was. They fed him. He grew strong again. He helped a woman with an injured arm. The tribe were pleased. Now he was one of them. He could stay with them as long as he liked.

He took the tribe to Burke's body in the desert. They wept. If they'd found Burke alive they'd have saved him, too . . .

***

No one in Melbourne knew what had happened to Burke and his team. Had they crossed Australia, or had they died? A rescue party was sent to find them.

Some weeks later they saw a man come out of some bushes. He wore part of a hat. He dropped to his knees when he saw them. He lifted his hands to the sky. He seemed to be praying. He was a white man.

'Who in the name of God are you?' asked a rescuer in surprise.

'I'm John King,' came the answer.

'King?' he asked.

'Yes sir. The last man alive. The others are all dead. But Burke and Wills . . . they made it.'

King fell on his knees and wept. It was a year and 25 days since he'd left Melbourne. He was now safe. The only one of the four to survive.

13

Finally...

A telegraph line was later built across Australia. But not along the route Burke, Wills, King and Gray had explored.

You can see Burke's statue in a park in Melbourne. He'd wanted to live for fame. It was sad he had to die for it. Burke and Wills are now seen as heroes.

If you'd like to find out more about Burke and Wills, visit the website:

http://www.davidreilly.com/australian_explorers/burke/burke_n_wills-easier.htm or

http://www.zoomwhales.com/explorers/page/b/burkewills.shtml

This book was inspired by *The Dig Tree* by Sarah Murgatroyd (Bloomsbury, 2002) and a variety of internet sites.

If you enjoyed this story, why not try this other NEW SPIRALS story about long and difficuly journeys:

Crash in the Jungle by Jim Alderson